Shadows of the Cross

Best Wishes to you,
Sister Gabriel.

Randy Dixon

Shadows of the Cross

Pencil Drawings by Randy Dixon
Reflections by Molly Roth

A Campion Book

Loyola University Press
Chicago

Loyola University Press
3441 North Ashland Avenue
Chicago, Illinois 60657

Cover and interior design by Nancy Gruenke
Cover art based on the stained glass windows of Arthur Stern
Cover pencil drawing by Randall Dixon

Library of Congress Cataloging-in-Publication Data

Roth, Molly DeSchryver
    Shadows of the cross / pencil drawings by Randall Dixon ;
reflections by Molly DeSchryver Roth.
        p.   cm.
    ISBN 0-8294-0810-X
    1. Jesus Christ—Passion—Poetry. 2. Stations of the Cross—Poetry.
3. Christian poetry, American. I. Dixon, Randall. II. Title.
PS3568.08545S63   1994
811'. 54—dc20   94-19568
                                                              CIP

This book is dedicated to Father Anthony DiRusso, a good friend who opened his heart and his church to my art. It is also dedicated to my wife, Chris, and our children, Cory and Emily, who were my models and inspiration.

—R. D.

This book is also dedicated to my brother, Brian, who stayed behind in Cambodia as a missionary when the Khmer Rouge began their autogenocide. These stations were a way for me to remember Brian and voice the grief I felt at his death, still sharp after twenty years.

—M. R.

Preface

I knelt with the rest of my fourth-grade class as altar boys poured sweet, heavy smoke into the air and Monsignor Luke led the stations of the cross. As we prayed, the stations came alive in a way the stylized pictures lining the church walls never had. In spite of my fascination, the incense and drone of prayers overwhelmed me. Though I could still hear my pastor's voice, I blacked out. I placed my head between my knees before I fainted, recovering in time to sing, "Let All Mortal Flesh Keep Silence."

Twenty years later, Randy Dixon and I were sitting over coffee after mass, with others from our choir, when he brought out his drawings of the stations of the cross. I expected the same kind of pictures I had seen as a child. Instead, I saw a series of pencil drawings that detailed the crucifixion starkly and compellingly. Randy had worked with Arthur Stern, of Arthur Stern Studios, and Karen Fishburn, a glass painter, to produce a series of stained-glass windows for Saint Mary's Parish in Lakeport, California. Karen had painted each station on glass, layering the ceramic frit, or glaze, to produce an image based on Randy's original drawing. Then, Arthur had placed each painted image in a larger window of stained glass with hand-bevelled prisms at the intersections of numerous glass crosses. He had used earth tones on one side of the church and blues and whites on the other to suggest earth and heaven. In 1990, the windows won an award of merit from the Interfaith Forum of Religious Art and Architecture (IFRAA).

A few years later, Randy expressed an interest in publishing his original drawings and asked me if I would write something to accompany them. My first thought was to write prayers and meditations. I tried, but they sounded preachy. When I took a second look at Randy's stations, I noticed that he had drawn each from a unique point of view. For instance, I had never before seen the washing of Pilate's hands from Pilate's visual point of view. For each of the stations, I asked myself, "Who is watching?" and tried to speak in that character's voice. At the same time, I knew the "characters" that arose were parts of me, rather than probable historical accounts of past peoples. I'm not at all sure what the real John would have thought or said, but I have nonetheless written what I would say *as* John.

I also found myself playing with the traditional image of Christ as light of the world. Here, he is the shadow that allows people to see God's light—he is the filtered light of a tomb, a dream of clouds, the dark presence within a halo. He takes unworthiness, darkness, and redeems it.

Randy and I also discussed the connections between past and present. He had drawn the stations as a contemporary way of seeing traditional images. For example, as Jesus is stripped in the tenth station, Randy drew him from directly above, as one would see a homeless person from above. I took this view a step further by connecting the dehumanizing point of view with

Preface (continued)

God's point of view, since God is often presented as someone high above us. Yet, God's point of view is also from within, which Christ lived to show and God recognizes in the poem. We hope that these pictures and poems will also encourage others to discover what the stations mean to them, to bridge the gaps between themselves and the way of the cross, as we have tried to do ourselves.

Finally, Randy and I would like to thank the following for their love and assistance: Chris Dixon, Jim Roth, Jack Stich, and Tina McMillan.

—Molly D. Roth, 1994

The cast of characters is as follows:

I. Pontius Pilate

II. A Pharisee

III. Mary, Jesus' Mother

IV. Mary Magdalene

V. A Shepherd/Carpenter

VI. Veronica

VII. A Shopkeeper

VIII. Jesus

IX. A Roman Guard

X. God

XI. A Man Who Nails People to the Cross

XII. The "Good Thief"

XIII. John

XIV. Joseph of Arimathea

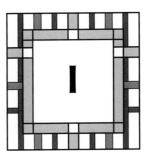

Wakes: Jesus Is Condemned to Death

I look down at the waves
that cross and parcel your face,
a mosaic of my indecision,
this silver bowl embracing
my life, the wakes of decisions made
and refused.

This net of diamonds,
sun-glinting web,
I cast
to submerge the truth,
drown it,
but your face remains whole—
I recognize its lines, what I cost you
written upon your skin.

Now the glare about your head blinds me
until I can only feel the bowl
press against my wrists.
I close my eyes and wonder
if I will ever again see the sun,
a sight made possible by your very shadow,
your face, gentling the truth
and my shame.

I long to sink
into the peace
of never having been born,
free at last of all nets,
to travel beneath the world,

away from
dirty streets
homeless children
wars of ignorance
blood-spattered women
subtle coersion
rape, incest
homophobia
blind racism—

your litany, as I try
to obliterate your face,
only to intensify the sun
in wave after wave
of my own denial.

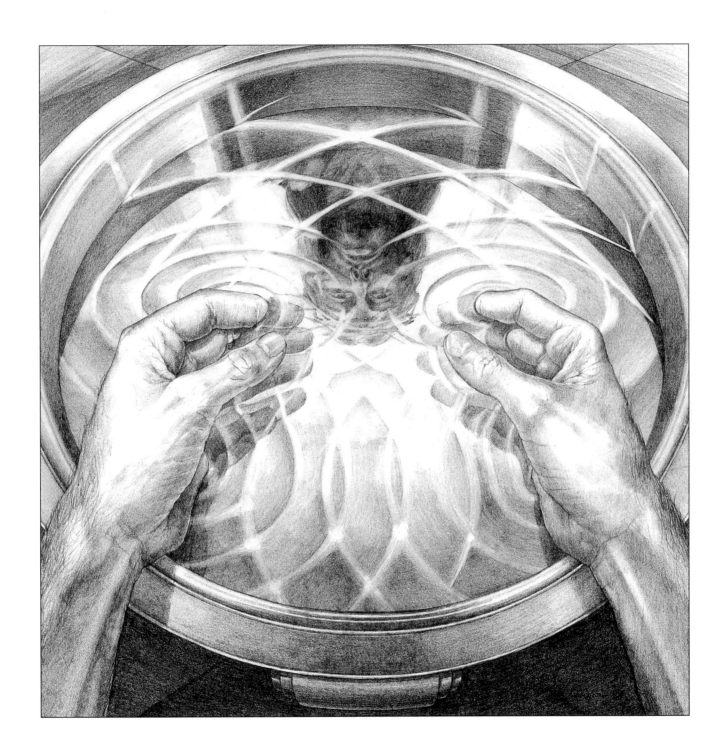

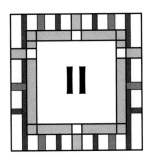

Dreaming of Clouds: Jesus Bears His Cross

Jesus! A whispered word—
to see you like this
almost breaks my heart.
I begin to pity you

until I remember the crime,
the blasphemy that struck our ears
and crazed us to righteousness
as you threatened to block the truth.

Our duty lies with the sun,
the truth, which you dared
to assume, as if any one man
could be God!

Those reports of your blazing face—
yes, we heard. Can you hear me?
You gaze straight ahead, your face so still,
you look like a part of the road.

Yes, we heard you had "cavorted"
with Elijah. News travels fast
to the just. How dare you
feast on the hopes of small people,

raise their expectations
until life could not meet them, then
leave us to pick up your pieces?
You will evaporate—

our sun, too strong for you and yours,
will suck the life from your lie,
as large as the log on your back
and as heavy for the deluded few.

Your yoke is no longer easy—
such drivel! And yet, at times,
I could almost believe you.
Thus, you must die.

Even now, you weigh like water—
dark clouds inside me,
burdened with a longing
too strong to destroy completely.

As a child, I relished these clouds,
the sweet foreboding, scent of
lightening, low rumbles, matched
only by my own heart—

then, whoosh! the wind would strike me
through my thin shirt, out of the
cool, dark shadow of clouds
too dangerous to touch—

such nonsense! The sun, this heat,
this wall blocking the air—
all have gone to my head!
So, why am I here?

(continued)

Dreaming of Clouds: Jesus Bears His Cross (continued)

Waiting for these guards to
strap you to your death,
experts at lashing, crossing
and recrossing the ties that bind.

I ought to strike you, but I squat
and wait for a forgiveness,
the burden of being the sun
suddenly too great for me,

and now you look at me,
and I see the sun in your eyes
reflected off my face
burn back toward my own heart,

still too great for me.
So I must leave, dreaming of clouds—
a foolish dream that will not die,
in spite of my best efforts.

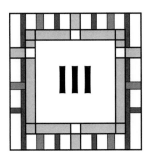

A Parting: Jesus Falls the First Time

My son—
the light dances so strangely
on these old walls—
the same light, same walls,
but so peculiar!

These shoulders, spears,
have parted just
enough, just in time, to reveal
you, a stone in the street, and
I, distant as the sun.

A brief, unmerciful flash,
and I spot you
between the legs of your father's sawhorse.

You have tripped,
and I notice the same light
cut across your motionless shoulder
through the shadows
of two wooden legs.

For an instant
nothing moves,
not even I.

Then a voice
shakes me from my disbelief.
I leap to see the wound,
to feel the warmth and pulse of your body.

I remember your father and I waited
until you opened your eyes
in the dark safety of a room—

our concern sparked at you
until we felt you again
and could cry with you.

You had run like a bright wind,
only to trip and fall
harder than a child deserves.

Now, your eyes are lost to me,
your body,
your life—

and the shoulders will close again,
the walls grow dark,
the spears be returned to their racks,
straight, shining, ready—

but tomorrow, my anger
will soak the sky as my disbelief—
the measure of my distance—
fills with Mary, John, Joseph,
like rain, their shoulders will flow together
to heal your void, a scar
ripped from the sun.

Your step
another mistake or not,
this distance is my best,
for now.

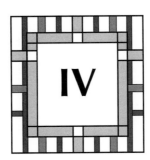

IV

Scour of Sand: Jesus Meets His Mother

I wish that old drunk would shut up!
Telling her to go home,
that it's not natural for her to be calm,
as if motherhood were measured in screams.
Guys like that used to keep me in business.
But not Jesus—he minded his own business—
and look what he got!

Listen, he's trying to come out of himself,
clear the haze of pain, of blood and sweat
to say, what was that?
"Hello, Mother."
I see the ripples around his mouth,
his smile, a shadow
set against the sadness for her pain.

My God! I can't take this—
did he save me,
bring my body and soul back together,
just so I could crumple back
into a dirty, empty shell?

I spot a woman behind him.
Or is she a ghost?
Pretty soon he'll be the ghost—
he'll know, then, if he doesn't already know,
what it's like to be a ghost.

Just last week, they stoned Miriam,
and here he is, dying.
I don't count on rescues, though I had one.
God doesn't owe me any favors.
I don't think Jesus counts on them, either,
not this time, anyway.

Even so, I wish he did—I think he's going to die,
and I want to die with him,
but I won't. He taught me that.

Instead, I'll burn with his death.
Not like the old days,
when I floated above it all,
my body a stone haunted by a hope
that he brought back to life.

Miriam never got the chance—
those bastards didn't even listen,
with their stinking breath
and fat hands held high,
ready to enjoy their latest kill!

So, now what do I hope for?
Ignore the men, use them the old way?
No. I am no longer a ghost
blown about from rock to rock:
I am the wind,
risen to scour every stone hefted in anger,
my song, the scream of sand
torn from the blood-soaked rocks
dead on the desert floor
until he came
and they shouted!

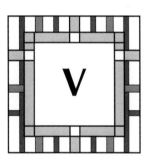

The Quality of the Wood: Jesus Is Helped by Simon

A fine piece of wood. What a waste!
See how even the grain is. Look,
there at the end. It'll have to be strong
to hold him up.

Wait, they've stopped. That guy—
Simon?—can't get it up on his shoulders.
Why doesn't that Jesus pick up the other end?
It's his cross, after all! You know, it's just like

that time you helped me build that fence—
for two hours, I struggled by myself—
two hours, dragging the heavy piles
up and around the back of the barn

until you stopped by. I should have known to
   ask,
but no, I had to do it all myself.
We finished the rest in half an hour—
I never thought to ask you.

They say his father was a carpenter,
so he must know about these things,
when to help and when not to help.
Now it looks like his help needs help.

But it's not my place, is it, to help.

I remember how we stood there,
   admiring our fence.
It let in air and light, but kept those sheep
   in at night
and the wolves out. A beauty!
Not like the mass burning along this road.

Remember, we sat and drank a few afterwards
as we wiped the sweat from our faces,
and the neighbors admired it, and my wife—
Some fence! The boys can climb it,
   but not that wolf!

Yes, a fine piece of wood, strong.
Too bad we can't help. What's that?
You want to help him? But he's a criminal!
OK, if you do it, I'll do it. Wouldn't mind

hefting that wood. Such a waste.
Anyway, I feel silly here on the ground
staring at the backs of his legs
white with sweat and light,

like that wall—burning, bare—
no air here. No, I'm not going soft!
But it looks like they don't need help.
Jesus has picked up the other end, after all.

I'll bet he appreciates the quality of the wood.

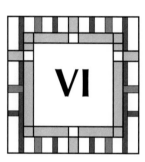

VI

Crazy with My Own Strength:
Veronica Wipes the Face of Jesus

—afraid
you wouldn't accept,
so I waited
until the sight of your face
compelled me to raise my hands
and this old cloth
that smelled of my own
hair, my damp head,

afraid, at first,
to offer this poor thing,
but when I felt your face
sink into my hands,
felt your entire body swoon,
your pain fall in folds
about my fingers,
I remembered my firstborn asleep on my breast,
the warm weight of young bodies,
my own ferocious strength in holding them.

Oh God!
I must let go.
You must die.

But even as they take you away,
I stand here and tremble
with my own power.

Now, the vicious ache,
not because you are gone,
but because I once held you.

I touch your life's weight
ever burned into me,
the cloth charged with your passion,

and I dance and dance,
crazy with my own strength.

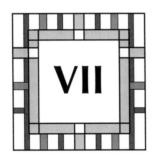

The Proper Authorities: Jesus Falls a Second Time

I see he has fallen
Down—how slow!
This event will never end.

Such a scene!
Scaring away
My best customers.

That poor fool.
I don't see why prisoners
Must face such an end.

The authorities
Must not have realized
The utter inefficiency

Of making such people shoulder
Such a weight
In such a weakened condition.

I think I'll write a letter,
No, wait, make a visit
To the proper authorities.

I will inform them
Of this outrage,
Tell them what to do.

I don't understand.
He just lies there.
He should just get it over with.

He cannot even
Stop his fall.
His face, I see, the blood.

So ugly! If truth is beauty
He should be killed
For the utter lie he represents.

The lies I've heard!
Women, men, even children
Embarrass me with themselves.

That soldier's kicking him.
That's what I'd do.
It's for his own good.

C'mon! Get up!
Let's get this over with!
You're ruining my business.

All the riff-raff
Blocking the street—
I'll report that, too!

We shouldn't have to
Put up with these spectacles—
Just kill them cleanly, quickly,

And let me get on with my business.

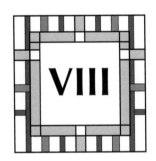

Ghosts: Jesus Speaks to the Women

Who is there?

mothers, sisters, daughters
ghosts that clean up after the world

I die for you
and our children
for me, a child—
for us all, children . . .
we all are children . . .

What?

She wants to hold me.
Please hold me!
I need you,
I need help.

No—
Don't go!
Let them stay!
"Weep for yourselves"

Yes.

"Don't weep for me,"
 you have to go back
 to your houses.
 Yes, anger,
 the brute who married you
 hit you again—the bruise
 shadowing your left cheek.

All at once,
 your pain focuses mine—
"Daughters of Jerusalem!
Weep not for me
but for your children, yourselves."
Your children—
we all deserve
a loving father,
brother, husband,
mother, sister,
wife.

Why am I here?
I can no longer
stand for it.

Papa!
Your gentle light pulls me
through this reasoning.
Shadows surface through the pain,
the lines of their faces.

But the sun makes ghosts of them,
erases each trail of feeling, thought—
so I must be consumed:
then, all may see the blaze in truth,
warmth in fire, truth in shadows . . .

I can no longer stand—

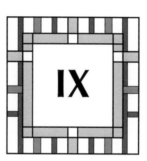

Just Orders: Jesus Falls a Third Time

Can you get up? I don't think he can hear me!
No, don't kick him—let him be!
I'll take care of this!

Jesus, Jesus. Get up.
We have to keep moving, you know.
We have our orders to keep the peace.

Just like that city in Macedonia—
So many people in the way.
We don't want a riot.

We thought they'd been evacuated.
You know, they should have been.
Somebody screwed up.

When we crashed through the gates,
They stood, massed in one place,
All those huddled women and children.

Of course we had to go through them.
We had no other choice.
They just crouched there, waiting.

C'mon! Get up, you stinking bastard!
I heard your mother was "in a family way"
Before your father married her, so

Why should you be any different?
They say you were,
But now look at you.

Poor bastard! Can't even hear me.
All you can see is your own shadow
And your burning hand, bent back.

What am I doing talking to you?
I said move it! Get up!
Just get it over with.

Get up, already! Just do it!
It's not so bad once you're through.
If you push too hard, maybe you'll die quickly,

Though I have my orders to keep you alive—
"Keep the prisoners alive" until you've hung,
To carry out the sentence.

Here, let me help you. Got my orders,
    you know?
Gotta keep this parade moving, you know?
Not my fault, just orders. That's it.

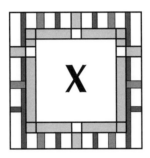

The Mirror: Jesus Is Stripped of His Garments

My son,
I see, as they strip you
to your last nakedness,
the homeless reduced to a spot.

Your body a dot,
I sign the world with you,
spend your blood's ink
over and again in lines of legato,
staccato—sweet, black, hard notes
strung along fissures
torn open once more.

You, the heart of a rose grown tight around me,
bloom to unwrap yourself into the world:
your damp scars fly through the parched air
to sing me like blood into the farthest heart.

I long to sing to you,
clothe you,
hold you,
touch your warm skin,
breathe your breath—
reduced to a speck,
my heart,
my precious one.

Your pain is mine,
your fear, mine,
your hope, mine:
I am at home.

Do not despair—
others will repeat our song,
their throats scored with longing for themselves,
unfurled in lines of such beauty
even those who cannot see
will begin to see, through our eyes:
the path you took to find me
ends with a mirror and a smile—
amazed, breath-taken.

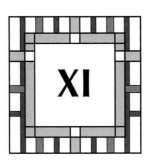

Tools: Jesus Is Nailed to the Cross

I hate this job.
Someone's gotta do it,
or so they say.

The soldiers won't do it,
so they hire me!
So why do I do it, anyway?

Most of all, I hate the screaming.
The blood doesn't bother me anymore.
Just the screaming.

This one's too tired to scream.
Sometimes they faint.
I like it when they faint.

This hammer's too small.
I like to get it done with one or two whacks,
better that way.

This puny thing will take forever,
though it's perfect for more delicate work,
tacking cloth onto a frame,

sails on that boat—
I loved sailing, in better times,
when I caught the most fish in my village.

Now, after the accident,
I can't do it anymore—
no legs to stand and cast the net,

so that's why I do this.
God took my legs, so now
I get to take other people's legs and arms.

Some justice.
God, I wish I could get used to the screams.
They bother me at night, sometimes,

but then, I just take out my bottle
and drink and drink
and all the screams disappear,

but then, little screams, babies,
return. I can hear them
inside the bottle.

I really need a better hammer.
This one's just not doing the job.
But I guess I'm stuck with it.

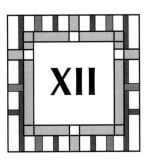

The Benefit of a Doubt: Jesus Dies on the Cross

Everyone, everything seems
so small from up here—
those women, their faces a blur.
That damn wall, with its
shade too short to reach me,
blocks the sweet, cool wind,
each brick a measure of my torture.

At least I don't have that ignoramus
telling me off—
"Hey! Leave him alone!"
He keeps at Jesus, keeps at him.
"Shut up! He doesn't deserve this!"

I know how the courts work.
They want you out of the way, and
Zip! You're in disgrace.
They can make the words say anything.
I should know. I can, too,
but I chose a different career,
just little crimes, really,
but big enough to get caught
at the wrong time, in the wrong place.

"Leave him—alone!"
I can barely speak.
My God! I'm dying!
And for what?
A lousy gamble that backfired.
I guess my luck's as bad as his,
no, not nearly as bad;
yet, those women weep for him.
I have no one, not even myself.

Oh, so philosophical! Here I hang,
the great prophet, ruminating
on the great mystery of my life.
It's so sad, I could laugh, if I could
breathe. OK, keep thinking,
use that useless wit of mine
that my father graced
with the back of his hand
to tarnish my silver tongue,
this tongue that threatens to gag me
like just desserts or deserts,
no one ever spells those right.

I could have been a scholar,
studied at Temple—
I could have sat there, richly robed,
listened to Jesus. I heard he didn't say much,
just threw their words in their faces.
My kinda guy.

Some stood up for him.
I wonder if I would have had the nerve.
No—and in a flash I see
I could have flicked at the population
like camel-drivers at flies,
drunk with the heat of power,
but instead, I hang dying—
the world's blessing.

Got to keep thinking.
He, that Jesus, still putting up with that slime.
Got no choice, I guess.

(continued)

They say Jesus spoke of love, of God as a Papa.
No wonder they hated him.

Listen. Now he's quiet.

He's seen me. He's looking
me right in the eyes I think
my mouth says, "Remember me."
Funny. Re-member. Remember.
In spite of it all, I cannot kill
that hope that burns in my throat.

The heat's twisted my mind—I see, in the haze,
my life, the rich robes sheltering him,
the words healing, my words—

Maybe I was wrong. Maybe
my father was wrong.
Silver-tongue loved a man,
hid it in his words,
no one knew but one or two,
but now, I can no longer see

as words fail me.

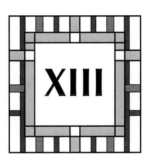

The Gift: Jesus Is Taken from the Cross

So, this is death—
stiff, awkward,
blank, but still warm.

She has finally felt it
after her shocked strength
lost its reason for being.

See how tenderly
she holds him,
she, who took in

every word against him,
every cruelty, every nasty look,
tried not to blame herself for his choice.

Even so, she must wonder
if she caused this. I know
I fear I caused it, somehow.

Look how she lies on that gape,
covers it with her body.
I envy her,

the release of such grief—
but if I cry, I'll break
into pieces. I'll die.

Funny—in a way, I want to die,
but I just can't.
His body wavers a million miles away

as I float on her wails,
her river of tears:
I am her boat,

like that boat Peter jumped clear out of—
I never knew that old man could move so fast,
his eyes bugging out at Jesus, on the water,

and Jesus just standing there, grinning,
as the rest of us burst out laughing in the boat,
and the storm passing, and light dancing
    on the water,

and my heart singing for this man
who made Peter skip along the waves,
who loved me clear through

like the sun striking down to the shore's bottom
to illuminate each golden stone and shell,
he pierced me—Oh God!

I just got what I prayed for.

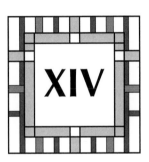

XIV

To See into Shadows: Jesus Is Laid in the Tomb

I stand in the darkness
of my tomb, now his—
he could have been my own son.

"A good time to prepare a tomb."
Who would have thought
my foresight would end so?

Now, these old fingers
straighten his beard,
wipe the last traces of blood away.

Everything is in order—
the linens prepared, oils bottled,
body washed, except for this spot of blood,

so stubborn, as if to say,
"Look! I really lived once!"
My poor Jesus! I am old—

how strange that you
would end up in my grave
as if you had died for me!

Only a haze of sun
filters into this tomb,
allowing me to see into shadows,

unlike the sharp light that
scorched you to ash, and I fear
I must face at the last.

Death smells strange, but sweet,
as I face your end—yet another change,
another step toward a light, I hope,

like the soft flow of mother's milk,
the evening breeze, silk,
scent of embers, honey cakes,

but I think I will have the courage
to walk through even the harshest light
to see you once more—

it's all the same light, the same road,
the same loving God who shines:
but you shone too widely for most.

Your face has grown too bright
as my eyes have adjusted to this dark place;
I must remember to rest them.

"All ready? Good. I'll be right out!"
Now I must return to the bright world
after one last touch. Goodbye—

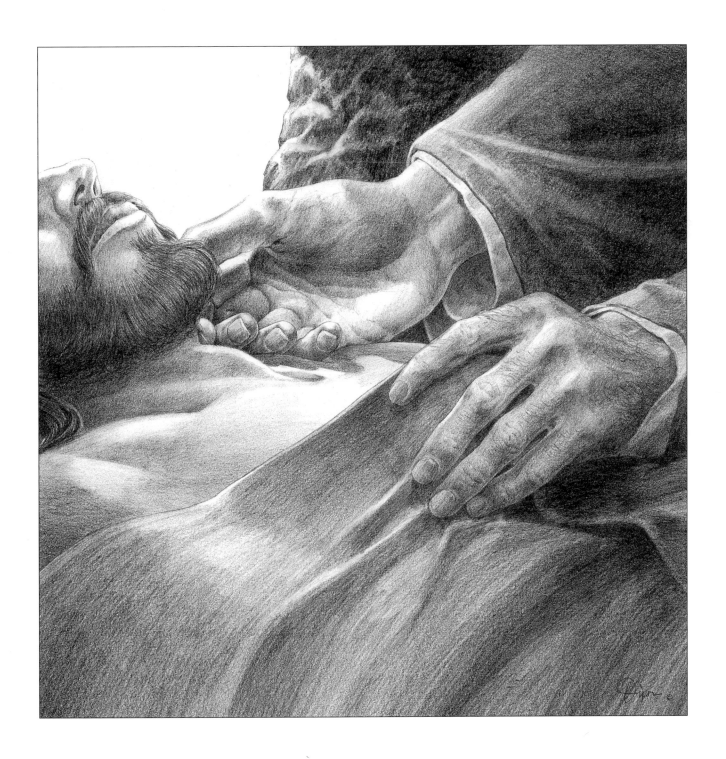